Security Valuation:

A Simple Introduction

Also by K.H. Erickson

Simple Introductions

Accounting and Finance Formulas
Applied Econometrics
Choice Theory
Corporate Finance Formulas
eBay
Econometrics
Economics
Environmental Economics
Financial Economics
Financial Risk Management
Game Theory
Game Theory for Business
International Relations
Investment Appraisal
Investment Formulas
Marketing Management Concepts and Tools
Mathematical Formulas for Economics and Business
Methods of Microeconomics
Microeconomics
Security Valuation

Security Valuation:

A Simple Introduction

K.H. Erickson

© 2016 K.H. Erickson

All rights reserved.

No part of this publication may be reproduced, stored in or introduced into a retrieval system, or transmitted in any form or by any means, including electronic, mechanical, photocopying, recording or otherwise, without the prior permission of the author.

Contents

1 Introduction	7
2 The Three-Step Valuation Process	**10**
2.1 Approaches to Security Valuation	10
2.2 Economy Analysis	13
2.3 Industry Analysis	18
2.4 Company Analysis	21
2.5 Support for the Three-Step Valuation Model	23
3 The Theory of Valuation	**25**
3.1 The Components of Valuation	25
3.2 Required Rate of Return	27
3.3 Stream of Returns	34
3.4 The Investment Decision	44
4 Bond and Preferred Stock Valuation	**47**
4.1 Bond Valuation	47
4.2 Preferred Stock Valuation	58
5 Discounted Cash Flow (DCF) Valuation	**61**
5.1 The Basics of DCF Valuation	61
5.2 Dividend Discount Model (DDM)	66
5.3 Present Value of Operating Free Cash Flow	84
5.4 Present Value of Free Cash Flow to Equity	92

6 Relative Valuation Models   **96**

6.1 The Basics of Relative Valuation   96

6.2 Price-to-Earnings (P/E) Ratio   99

6.3 Price-to-Cash Flow (P/CF) Ratio   101

6.4 Price-to-Book (P/B) Ratio   102

6.5 Price-to-Sales (P/S) Ratio   103

1 Introduction

As the name suggests, security valuation attempts to place a monetary value on securities, which are defined in finance terms as any tradable financial asset. Security valuation is very important to investors, as the process can be used to estimate the intrinsic value of an asset, which can then be compared to the current market price of that asset. If the estimated intrinsic value of an asset is greater than its current market price then the asset is currently undervalued, and it makes sense for an investor to buy it, under the rational expectation that the market price will soon rise to reflect the security's true value, thereby generating a profit for the investor. But if the estimated intrinsic value of an asset is less than its current market price then the asset is currently overvalued, and the investor shouldn't buy it, due to the rational expectation that the market price will soon fall to reflect the security's true value, which would generate a loss for any investor.

Securities are usually divided into two categories: equity securities and debt securities. Equity securities are those tradable financial assets which give the holder a claim on the assets and earnings of a company, and an example would be common stock shares of a corporation. As the name equity suggests, equity securities are a fair and impartial financial instrument, and give investors a fair share of a company's market value. If the price of a company's shares rises then an investor holding equity (shares) will see the value of their investment rise accordingly, while if the price of a company's shares falls an investor holding equity will see the value of their investment fall accordingly. Debt securities are those tradable financial assets which require a fixed payment to be paid to the holder, and examples would be government or corporate bonds, or mortgages. An investor holding debt securities will receive a fixed payment (the principal) on the maturity date of the debt, and will also often receive interest payments (the coupon) over the life of the debt.

There are two different methods of security valuation; a top-down three-step approach, and a bottom-up stock picking approach. The former first examines the state of the overall economy, then an industry, and finally the features of an individual company, based on the idea that the state of the wider economy and a company's industry will naturally affect the value of a company and its stock. In contrast the bottom-up stock picking approach believes an investor can pick out undervalued stocks, irrespective of the state of the industry and economy. The three-step approach is usually more popular, and the reason why is detailed along with the relevant factors in the next chapter.

With a three-step valuation process selected and justified, the next step is to understand the theory of valuation. The valuation of an asset has three components, each of which are given separate sections. The most obvious component is the stream of returns associated with the asset, which is the cash flow an investor will receive if they buy the asset. This stream of returns is decided by the growth rate of the asset's earnings, and factors determining this growth rate are detailed with an explanation of the DuPont System. But an investor is not motivated by cash flow directly, and what matters most is the value the cash flow represents. This is determined with the second component of asset valuation, the required rate of return, which discounts a future stream of returns into a more realistic present value, based on the uncertainty of the cash flows, and the other investment opportunities on offer. The third component of asset valuation is the decision to invest or not, based on the findings of the valuation.

Valuation moves from process and theory to practice, with sections applying asset valuation to bonds and preferred stock. Common stock valuation is more complicated, and it is tackled in two ways which should be seen as complementary. Discounted cash flow valuation focuses on company analysis, and different sections explain dividend, operating free cash flow, and free cash to equity present value models. Relative valuation focuses more on comparative industry and economy analysis, and separate sections outline price-to-earnings, price-to-cash flow, price-to-book value, and price-to-sales models.

2 The Three-Step Valuation Process

2.1 Approaches to Security Valuation

As explained in the introduction, there are two approaches to security valuation: a top-down three-step approach and a bottom-up stock picking approach. The top-down approach believes that the state of the overall economy will affect the performance of an industry, which will in turn affect the performance of the companies which make up that industry. Therefore adherents to the top-down three-step approach will examine the economy, the industry, and the company together in the security valuation process. The bottom-up approach focuses only on the company however, believing that stock picking those assets with an intrinsic value above their current market price doesn't require an analysis of the state of the economy or industry performance.

Investors following a bottom-up approach will not necessarily ignore differences in industries or in the current state of the economy completely. They may take account of differences in industries and ensure their portfolio represents a diverse mix of industries to reduce their risk exposure, and may take note of the current state of the economy by including the national rate of interest as a risk-free asset to secure a return with no risk. Investment in a risk-free asset and portfolio diversification to reduce diversifiable risk are certainly good ideas, and are both empirically supported strategies for investors. But there is also evidence that the state of the economy and a company's industry should be included in the individual security valuation process itself, and that the top-down three-step approach to security valuation is therefore superior to the bottom-up purely stock picking valuation approach.

If the economy is doing well and there is a significant economic expansion, and the overall industry of a company is doing well, then it is reasonable to assume that the average company in that industry will also be doing well. Its market value and therefore market price will be on an upward trend, as will be the value of the company's assets. But if the economy is doing badly and there is a major economic recession, and the overall industry of a company is doing badly, then it is reasonable to assume that the average company in that industry will also be doing badly. Its market value and therefore price will be on a downward trend, as will the value of the company's assets. This simple generalisation suggests the potential folly of the bottom-up security valuation approach. Even if it is able to identify those company stocks which have undervalued market prices, if that company's industry and the overall economy are in a downward trend then instead of the market price rising (to its intrinsic value) as expected, the market price may fall further. Those investors following the top-down three-step valuation approach would have been predicted this as they examined the state of the economy and the company's industry, and avoided those stocks accordingly. But those investors following a bottom-up stock picking approach would not have paid attention, and would have made a poor investment in a stock heading downwards, causing them a loss.

This is only a theoretical example of why the three-step approach to security valuation is superior, and a detailed analysis using practical examples makes the case even stronger. The following sub-sections do this and show why a three-step method is the best choice, and how the general state of the economy, industry factors, and company factors, will affect the valuation of a company's financial assets.

2.2 Economy Analysis

A government's fiscal policy for the economy can have a significant impact on companies, and tax increases on income, or goods such as petrol (gasoline), alcohol or cigarettes will all reduce consumers' disposable income, reducing the amount of money they have to spend on a company's products. On the other hand tax cuts or tax credits on income or the aforementioned goods will increase consumers' disposable income, increasing the amount of money they have to spend on a company's products. Government increases or decreases in spending throughout the economy will also have an impact on companies. For example, reduced spending on national defence will worsen the prospects for defence companies, while increased spending on national infrastructure will improve the prospects for construction companies. On top of this government spending is associated with a multiplier effect. And increased government spending on the infrastructure of a national economy, for example, will not only improve the prospects and wealth for the workers and material suppliers of construction companies, but also those companies whose goods and services they will in turn spend this increased wealth on. All of this shows that what happens in the economy will have a major impact on a company, and that a bottom-up security valuation approach is wrong to ignore it.

The monetary policy a government sets for a national economy will also have an impact on a company. An expansionary monetary policy that increases the growth rate of the money supply (i.e. printing more money, or quantitative easing for an electronic version of this) will increase the supply of funds for all companies to use for working capital and business expansion. Alternatively, a restrictive monetary policy that reduces the growth rate of the money supply, such as raising market interest rates, will raise the cost of borrowing for both companies themselves, and also for consumers who would be their customers, worsening the business outlook for a company.

Looking beyond a government's fiscal and monetary policy to economy influences beyond a government's direct control, the level of inflation in an economy will also have a clear effect on companies. The last paragraph noted how the market interest rates set by government can affect a company, with a higher interest rate making it more expensive and therefore difficult for a company or its potential customers to borrow needed money, while a lower interest rate makes it less expensive and therefore easier to borrow. But the interest rate set by government is of course only the nominal interest rate, with the real interest rate that companies and customers will face determined by both this and the inflation rate, as the real interest rate = nominal interest rate − inflation rate. A company can also be affected by unexpected changes in the inflation rate, which can throw a company's plans off track and reduce both their growth and their potential for innovation.

The economies of other countries can also have an effect on companies. The interest rate and rate of inflation in foreign countries relative to their own country will affect the international trade prospects for a company, affecting both the cost of borrowing for potential customers in other countries, and the relative prices and therefore perceived value of a company's products. Currency exchange rates will also be affected by the relative state of national economies, and this exchange rate will determine the cost and therefore prospects for a company's product exports, and also the cost of buying the inputs a firm requires to operate its business. The overall trend of imports against exports determines the trade balance between countries, which will in turn determine the state of a national economy and define the type of monetary and fiscal policies a government will use, and as just noted this will affect the business prospects for a company.

The stability of a national economy, or the lack of stability, can also have a big impact on companies. A stable economy with strong institutions which can be relied upon to enforce the rule of law is a safe place to do business, and a safe place for investors to invest in, which is good for a company. On the other hand, a war torn country or a country with political instability may not offer a reliable and stable business environment, or protect investments, and will therefore hinder a company.

Overall, macroeconomic policies and developments appear to have a clear impact on a company, and this supports the idea of using the top-down three-step valuation process which starts with an examination of the state of national economies, in place of the stock-picking valuation approach which ignores this. In terms of how to incorporate the relative states of national economies into the process of stock valuation, this can be achieved with a higher or lower national asset allocation in a global portfolio.

For example, before an analysis of the state and likely future prospects of national economies was taken into account, the overall market value of country A may be 1.5 times that of country B in relative terms. This would suggest that 40% of an investor's money should be put in country B, and 60% of an investor's investment money (1.5 times as much) should be put in country A. But if an analysis of national economies and macroeconomics revealed a major economic upturn and boom was imminent in country A, while a major downturn and recession was forecast to hit in the very near future in country B, then these weightings would be changed according to the three-step valuation approach. Country A may then have, for example, a far higher 80% of investor money weighting, while country B may then have a far lower 20% weighting in the portfolio. And if a minor economic upturn was expected in country A in place of a major economic upturn and boom, and a minor economic downturn was expected in country B in place of a major downturn and recession, then the respective changes in portfolio wealth weightings would be less. Country A's weighting would be raised less, to 70% of total portfolio wealth for example, while country B's weighting would be reduced less to 30% of total portfolio wealth.

2.3 Industry Analysis

Once national economic analysis has been performed the next step of the three-step valuation approach is industry analysis, to determine which global industries are likely to succeed or struggle in the economic environment forecasted for different countries. Some industries, known as cyclical industries, fare far better than average industries in economic upturns and booms, but fare far worse than average industries in economic downturns and recessions. While other industries, known as noncyclical industries, do not see much of an increase in prospects during an economic upturn, but also not much of a decline in an economic downturn.

The car industry is an example of a cyclical industry, and if macroeconomic analysis had forecasted an economic upturn for a major national economy then the global car industry would make a good investment, as the economic upturn can be expected to make large numbers of people wealthier, and see more people spend some of this wealth on buying new cars. However, if macroeconomic analysis had forecast an economic downturn for a major national economy then the cyclical car industry would make a poor investment, as the downturn would be expected to make large numbers of people poorer, with less money to spend on buying nonessential luxury items such as new cars. In the case of a predicted economic downturn a noncyclical industry, such as the retail food industry, would make a better investment. Even in the middle of an economic downturn where people have less money necessities such as retail food (i.e. non restaurant food) will always be in high demand, and therefore sales of retail food should be steady and reliable to make the industry a safe investment.

As well as revealing the prospects for an economic upturn or downturn, effective macroeconomic analysis will have also noted government regulations, and demographic trends, as the state of these factors will help to understand and forecast economic performance. And therefore industry analysis will in turn reveal the industries which are likely to prosper and are worthy of investment, which are those industries with looser or supportive regulations and more favourable government policies, and industries serving expanding demographics. It will also reveal those industries likely to struggle and not worth investment, which are the industries with heavier or restrictive regulations and less favourable government policies, and industries which serve demographics which are declining in size or spending power.

The industry analysis noted may help an investor to understand which industries to consider, and simply observing an industry's changing performance in a shifting global economic environment may also offer insights into productive industries. It is important for an investor to conduct industry analysis before company analysis, and to determine those industries likely to do well in the near future before selecting specific companies to invest in, because as noted earlier, the performance of an industry will be an indicator for the performance of the average company in that industry. Few companies will do well in a poorly performing industry, and even the best company may be a poor investment. A randomly chosen company in a well performing industry is likely to be a better investment. And this again supports the idea of the three-step valuation approach to stock selection, with the top-down order of economy analysis being followed by industry analysis, and finally company analysis.

2.4 Company Analysis

Once an industry's outlook has been forecast as being good by industry analysis the next and final step is to perform company analysis, as investors analyse how the performance of individual companies compares to that of other firms in their industry. This analysis is undertaken using the publicly available financial ratios and cash flow values of a company, and the cash flow values reveal the relative inward and outward revenue streams of different firms, while financial ratios reveal the relative profitability, efficiency, liquidity, and debt levels of different firms. The financial ratios and cash flow values of different companies in an industry reveal their relative past performance and current position, which suggests their likely future prospects.

Once company analysis data has been acquired for different firms in an industry it is put into one of several possible valuation models, along with variables accounting for industry and economy data, in accordance with the three-step valuation process. Naturally it is essential that all of these three steps, the economy analysis, industry analysis, and company analysis, are performed correctly, as a valuation model is only as reliable as the data inputs it relies upon. The valuation model used will give an estimation of the intrinsic value of a company's stock, which can then be compared to the current market price of that company's stock. If the valuation model calculates the intrinsic value of a security as above its current market price then the security is undervalued, and is a worthwhile investment, but if the intrinsic value is calculated as below the market price then the security is overvalued, and is not a worthwhile investment.

The best and most profitable stock for an investor may not be from the best and most profitable company in an industry, as that company's stock may be overpriced and overvalued, and a poor investment. Economy analysis, industry analysis, and company analysis are therefore not used directly to select which securities to invest in, and are only the tools used to conduct an accurate valuation of a security's intrinsic value, which is then compared to its current market price to allow an informed investment decision. Once an investor has determined the securities worthy of investment then they can make their decision, based upon the relationship and correlation with other assets in the investor's portfolio.

2.5 Support for the Three-Step Valuation Model

The three-step valuation approach is supported by academic studies, which find that both the performance of the aggregate market economy, and a company's industry, have a significant effect on both a company's earnings and the rate of return of a company's stock. And the three-step approach to valuation is also consistent with the asset allocation decision process which investors will follow. The asset allocation decision sees investors decide on how much of their portfolio value to invest in each country's national economy, which industries (within a country) to invest in based upon those expected to perform best in the forecasted economic environment, and how the investor will divide their portfolio wealth between different types of assets based upon their relative risks and returns. And if investors allocate their investment wealth into assets based upon economy, industry, and asset risk-return factors, it follows that the valuation of those assets should also be based on economy, industry, and asset risk-return factors, via economy analysis, industry analysis, and company analysis respectively, according to the three-step top-down valuation process.

With the selection of the top-down three-step valuation approach explained and justified, the next step is to explain how its three steps of economy analysis, industry analysis, and company analysis affect the valuation of assets. The next section tackles this issue, and looks into the theory of valuation.

3 The Theory of Valuation

3.1 The Components of Valuation

The last section determined the top-down three-step valuation approach to be the superior method to value securities, and this approach involves combining economy analysis, industry analysis, and company analysis to value the three theoretical components of any asset valuation model. These three theoretical components are the stream of returns, the required rate of return, and the investment decision.

The first component is the stream of returns for a security, also known as the cash flow stream or profit stream, which is simply the inflows and outflows of money which are expected to be associated with a security over the time period it is held. Due to the time value of money, where a sum of money is worth less to an investor if received in the future than if that same sum of money was received today, due to foregone interest / inflation / uncertainty over the future, money received in the future must be discounted to allow an accurate comparison with that money received today. And the discount rate which makes future expected return streams and current return streams equivalent is known as the required rate of return, the second component of any valuation model. Finally, the third component of any valuation model is the investment decision, which compares the intrinsic value of a security (the sum of the stream of returns discounted at the required rate of return, according to the time they are expected to be received / sent) with its current market price, to ascertain if the investment is worthwhile.

Irrespective of which valuation model is chosen from a range of possible alternatives, the valuation is only possible only once these three theoretical components have been estimated and valued. A valuation model is only as good as the inputs put into it, and therefore a proper and accurate calculation of these components is essential. The next three sub-sections look into each component in turn to understand exactly how they are derived.

3.2 Required Rate of Return

The stream of returns associated with an asset over the period it will be held means nothing to an investor, unless they know how to make returns received at different future time periods equivalent and comparable, according to the time value of money principle. Without this step an investor can't accurately compare different assets with different return streams, and assess them to determine the superior investment. Therefore the first thing an investor will need to do is determine the discount rate, which is the interest rate the future returns of an investment must be discounted by to make them equivalent to returns received from an investment today in the present. As an investor operates in the present and not the future they will of course be looking at the discount rate from the opposite direction, and they must determine the rate of interest required to make current returns equal to future returns, which is known as the required rate of return (often denoted as 'k'). As they are the same thing but looked at from different directions, the required rate of return for an investment will always equal the discount rate for an investment.

Several factors come together to determine the required rate of return for an investment. The first is the real risk-free rate of return (RRFR) for an economy, which is the actual (as opposed to the nominal) rate of return which is available for investors with no risk whatsoever. The real risk-free rate of return is the absolute minimum rate of return an investor will require from an investment opportunity, as if an investment's rate of return was lower an investor would be better off forgoing the investment opportunity and opting for the risk-free asset instead. This real risk-free rate of return will depend upon the real growth rate of the economy, and invested capital would be expected to grow at least as fast as the economy grows. Note that 'the economy' here refers to home economy of the investor in question, as the real risk-free rate of return will be the real risk-free rate in an investor's home country (cross border transactions are never risk-free), and therefore the economy deciding that real risk-free rate of return must also be from the investor's home country.

The second factor affecting the required rate of return for an investment is the expected rate of inflation, $E(I)$, for the holding period of an investment. The inflation rate is important as it can be used together with the real risk-free rate of return to give the nominal risk-free rate of return (NRFR). While investors are interested in the actual and real risk-free rate of return for an investment, which accounts for inflation to make sure an investor's purchasing power is not eroded, it is the nominal risk-free rate of return which will be quoted for an investment and what an investor will operate with directly. And this nominal rate of return is therefore required to calculate the required rate of return for an investor. To find the nominal risk-free rate of return from the real risk-free rate and the expected rate of inflation, the following formula can be used:

Nominal rate of return = Real rate of return + Inflation rate

And accordingly the real rate of return can be found by rearranging the formula:

Real rate of return = Nominal rate of return − Inflation rate

A third and final factor affecting the required rate of return is the risk-premium (RP) associated with an investment. And with the other two factors of the inflation rate and real-risk free rate of return, and the nominal risk-free rate they create, the same across investments, it is ultimately the risk premium which will determine the required rate of return for alternative investments. The risk premium (RP) is the additional rate of return (i.e. the premium) an investor requires, over and above the nominal risk-free rate of return (NRFR), in order to be willing to take on an investment, and when the two are summed they reveal the investor's required rate of return (k):

$$k = NRFR + RP$$

The risk premium for an investment asset depends upon the level of uncertainty (i.e. risk) of returns or cash flow associated with an investment. A greater uncertainty of returns will result in a greater risk premium being set for an investment, while a lower uncertainty of returns will result in a lower risk premium for an investment. The level of uncertainty and risk associated with an investment asset, and therefore the level of the risk premium, will depend on the scale of several factors. And as the scale of these factors are likely to vary on company, industry, and economy lines, there is support for using the three-step valuation model to investigate all factors affecting the risk premium. Using the alternative stock-picking approach to determine the risk premium would ignore industry and economy sources of risk and uncertainty for an investment, generating an inaccurate risk premium and a broken valuation model. And this would cause an investor to make poor judgements in their investment decisions.

Internal sources of risk for an investment asset are the level of business risk (the possibility that the asset's company suffers lower than expected profits), financial risk (the asset's company is unable to secure the financial resources to operate), and liquidity risk (a company's financial resources are tied down and can't be used to meet short-term cash needs). Other internal sources of risk for a company and its assets are country risk (the possibility that investing or lending in a country's assets may become less profitable, due to potential changes in the business environment of that country), and exchange rate risk (a company makes transactions with a foreign company in a foreign currency, and movements in relative currency values work against the first company and its assets). For example, the value of the foreign currency may increase relative to the company's own country's currency, making it more expensive for the company to buy the foreign company's products and services. Or alternatively the value of the foreign currency may fall relative to the value of the company's own currency, making it harder for the company to sell its products which have become relatively more expensive for foreign companies.

External and market sources of risk and uncertainty for companies and their assets are a matter of debate. It is widely accepted that the inherent, systematic, non-diversifiable market risk (i.e. beta) of an asset is a source of uncertainty, and greater systematic risk will raise the risk premium an investor requires. Other common assumed sources of market risk relate to a firm's size and its book value to market value ratio relative to other firms in the market, with smaller companies and companies with a higher book-to-market ratio considered to come with greater risk. Smaller companies lack the resources of larger companies and therefore are more vulnerable to collapsing under the strain of the internal risk sources noted earlier. And companies with a higher book value (i.e. accounting value of assets) relative to their market value (market capitalization, the stock price multiplied by the total number of shares) are considered to have greater risk as they are under-priced by the market, relative to other companies. The implication is that in order to under-price the assets the market must believe such companies are poorly run and that their resources won't be used properly, hence the greater risk of investing in these assets. On the other hand companies with a lower book-to-market value are considered to have lower risk, as they are over-priced by the market relative to other companies. The implication being that the market must have information to justify that over-pricing, such as that the company is well run and its resources will be used more efficiently than other companies.

Note that this situation of undervalued and overvalued assets here is different to that mentioned earlier in this book, in the company analysis section of the three step valuation process chapter. Here the analysis only looks at the accounting book value of a company's assets relative to the market price, and factors about the performance of the company using those assets are missing. The market is therefore a useful source of additional information on a company, and the market's apparent relative under or overvaluation of assets may give investors an insight into the relative risk associated with different companies' assets. But earlier on in this book the analysis was based on a complete investigation into all factors affecting a company's value, and the market price was therefore not considered a source of additional information on risk or anything else, but something to compare an intrinsic value asset valuation with.

3.3 Stream of Returns

The stream of expected returns for a security is the incoming and outgoing streams of money forecasted over the time a security is held. There are several factors to be noted when valuing an asset's stream of returns. First, there is of course the size of the in and out cash flows and the amounts of money going in each direction. Next there is the time pattern over which these return streams occur, as this will affect the level of discounting required (at the required rate of return) to make future returns equivalent to current returns. Third, the relative uncertainty of the cash flow returns must be noted, as the forecasted amounts may not materialise, especially if they are due to occur far into the future. This uncertainty of the stream of returns will be accounted for by changing the required rate of return as will be explained later. Finally, there is the different forms which the returns and profits stream takes over a time period, such as cash flows, earnings, dividends, interest payments, etc. Even if returns are of the same size, occurring at the same time, and holding the same level of uncertainty, they can't be treated the same if they come in different forms, as different valuation models exist for dividends, operating cash flows, preferred stock, and so on.

One of the major determining factors for both the size and the timing of returns is the growth rate of returns, and therefore determining the growth rate is an essential part of modelling the stream of returns for an asset. But as returns come in different forms, as just noted, several different growth rates are relevant. Earnings, cash flow, and dividends growth rates will all affect the stream of returns associated with an asset differently, with earnings representing the amount of money a firm makes, cash flow representing when a firm's earnings are actually paid, and dividends being the amount of earnings paid out to shareholders of the firm's assets.

The expected growth rate of dividends is determined by the growth rate of earnings, and the proportion of earnings which are paid out as dividends, otherwise known as the payout ratio. The payout ratio can be calculated by dividing the dividends declared by a firm for a period (which creates a liability for the firm to make the associated payments), by the firm's operating income after taxes for that same period:

Payout ratio
= Dividends declared / Operating income after taxes

If the proportion of earnings paid out as dividends remains constant over time then dividends and earnings will have the same growth rate, no matter what the proportion of earnings paid out as dividends. This can be shown with a numerical example. If earnings are currently £100 per year, then a 10% earnings growth rate (i.e. £100 now in year 0, £110 after year 1, £121 after year 2), combined with a constant 0.5 (50%) payout ratio, gives a 10% per year dividend growth rate (i.e. £50 now in year 0, £55 after year 1, £60.5 after year 2). And the dividends and earnings growth rates will remain equal even if the proportion of earnings paid out as dividends changes to a different constant payout ratio, of for example 0.05 (5%). Earnings of £100 now in year 0, £110 after year 1, and £121 after year 2 (i.e. a 10% growth rate per year again), combined with a 5% payout ratio, gives a £5 dividend now in year 0, a £5.50 dividend after year 1, and a £6.05 dividend after year 2 (i.e. also a 10% growth rate).

However, if the proportion of earnings paid out as dividends (i.e. the payout ratio) changes over time then the earnings growth rate and dividends growth rate will differ. If a firm increases its payout ratio then dividends will grow faster than earnings over the period of the payout increase, and if a firm alternatively decreases its payout then dividends will grow slower than earnings for a period. But a disparity between earnings and dividends growth rates can only continue for a limited period of time, as the payout increases or decreases driving such a disparity can't last forever. The dividend payout ratio can't keep increasing indefinitely as dividends are paid out from earnings, and the payout ratio can never exceed beyond 100% of earnings. The dividend payout ratio also can't decrease forever, as it can't go any lower than a 0% payout ratio, where zero dividends will be paid out from earnings. Changes in the payout ratio are therefore only considered a short-term phenomenon, and over the long-run there is thought to be relative stability in the payout ratio, and an absence of any long-term increase trend or decrease trend. With a relatively stable payout ratio over the long-run, the difference between the earnings growth rate and dividend growth rate is limited over the long-run.

A relatively stable payout ratio in the long-run, with the earnings and dividends growth rates more or less equal, simplifies the factors determining the expected growth rate of dividends. Earlier the dividend growth rate was said to be determined by the growth rate of earnings and the proportion of earnings paid out as dividends (the payout ratio). But with the payout assumed fairly stable in the long-run changes in the dividend growth rate can be said as being caused primarily by changes in the growth rate of earnings. The growth rate of earnings is therefore the key growth rate affecting the stream of returns of an asset, as it drives dividends, earnings, and also (intuitively) cash flow (of earnings).

The growth rate of earnings (g) is determined by two factors. First is the retention rate of earnings, which is the percentage of net earnings (earnings after tax) a firm retains instead of paying out as dividends. The retention rate is a factor in the growth rate of earnings as earnings which are not paid out as dividends can be reinvested in other investment opportunities, raising a firm's potential sustainable growth level. This retention rate is the opposite of the payout ratio just explained, and can be found by subtracting the payout ratio from 1. Therefore if the payout ratio for a firm was 0.20 (i.e. a firm pays out 20% of its earnings as divvidends), then that firm's retention rate would be 0.80 (i.e. the firm retains 80% of its earnings), as $1 - 0.20 = 0.80$.

$$\text{Retention rate} = 1 - \text{Payout ratio}$$

$$\text{Retention rate} = 1 - (\text{Dividends declared} / \text{Operating income after taxes})$$

The second factor in the growth rate of earnings is the rate of return of the firm's equity capital. This factor follows on logically from the first factor, the retention rate of earnings, as when a firm retains (and then reinvests) some of its earnings they become part of the firm's equity and raise its value. And it is the rate of return of the firm's equity capital, the rate of return on the reinvestment opportunities, which will then determine the extent to which the firm's equity and earnings grow.

Putting the two factors together shows that the growth rate of earnings (g) is determined by the retention rate of earnings (RR) multiplied by the return on equity (ROE):

$$g = \text{Retention rate} * \text{Return on equity}$$

$$g = RR * ROE$$

This equation reveals that there are two ways for a firm to increase its earnings growth rate, g (and with it the dividends growth rate, and cash flow growth rate, as noted earlier). First, a firm could increase its retention rate, which is the same as lowering its dividend payout ratio. However, as noted earlier the dividend payout ratio can't be lowered indefinitely, and once 100% of earnings are retained the percentage of earnings retained can no longer be used to increase the growth rate of earnings. Financial theory suggests that a firm should retain earnings for reinvestment so long as the reinvestment is worthwhile, and generates an expected rate of return which exceeds the firm's cost of capital, the opportunity cost of the investment and the rate of return which could have been earned if the earnings were used elsewhere.

The second way for a firm to increase its earnings growth rate is to increase its return on equity (ROE), and therefore the driving factors of the ROE are worth investigation. These are detailed in the DuPont System.

DuPont System

ROE or return on equity is a shortening of the full name, return on shareholders' equity. This is the percentage return on a firm's equity (i.e. firm value, which includes preferred and common stock, paid-in capital, and all retained earnings), and can be found by dividing a firm's net income by shareholders' equity:

ROE = Net income / Shareholders' equity

The DuPont System breaks this formula down into three parts, and in doing so notes the three factors which drive a firm's return on equity, ROE. This DuPont system requires three modifications to the above formula.

First, the ROE formula above is multiplied by 1, and then by 1 again. This is acceptable as it clearly doesn't change the formula or add anything new to the equation, but it is desirable as it sets the equation up for later steps:

ROE = Net income / Shareholders' equity
= (Net income / Shareholders' equity) * 1 * 1

Second, the number 1 in the above equation is replaced by something which equals 1. The first number 1 is replaced by (Net sales / Net sales), which clearly equals one as the numerator (top) and denominator (bottom) are identical and cancel each other out. And the second number 1 in the equation is replaced by (Total Assets / Total assets), which also cancels out to equal one. The result is shown below:

ROE = Net income / Shareholders' equity
= (Net income / Shareholders' equity)
* (Net sales / Net sales) * (Total Assets / Total assets)

Third and finally, denominators are moved around. This is permissible as it doesn't change the equation, because the various factors are all multiplied by each other. An example can prove that moving denominators around doesn't change the equation if factors are multiplied by each other. (1/2) * (2/5) = 1/5, and switching denominators gives the same result as (1/5) * (2/2) = 1/5 too. With this proven we can go back to the ROE = Net income / Shareholders' equity equation, and rearranging denominators gives the following result:

ROE = Net income / Shareholders' equity
= (Net income / Net sales) * (Net sales / Total assets)
* (Total assets / Shareholders' equity)

This new equation reveals that a firm's return on equity, ROE, is comprised of three different ratios: net profit margin, total asset turnover, and equity multiplier:

(Net income / Net sales) = Net profit margin
(Net sales / Total assets) = Total asset turnover
(Total assets / Shareholders' equity) = Equity multiplier

And putting these three ratios back into the ROE equation gives:

ROE = Net profit margin * Total asset turnover * Equity multiplier

And the fact that a firm's ROE is comprised of these three ratios reveals the three different ways a firm can increase its return on equity. One, it can increase its net profit margin, which requires that the firm becomes more profitable. Two, a firm can increase its total asset turnover, which requires that the firm becomes more efficient and uses its assets more efficiently. And third, a firm could increase its equity multiplier. All of a firm's assets must be financed by equity (from a firm's assets) or by debt (from assets not held by the firm), and the higher the equity multiplier the greater the proportion of a firm's assets that are financed by debt. Therefore to raise ROE by increasing the equity multiplier a firm should increase its financial leverage, by raising the proportion of its assets which are financed by debt and not equity. This gives the final DuPont system return on equity equation, which shows the three components (along with the retention rate) which a firm can try to change to increase its earnings growth rate, and with it the dividend growth rate and cash flow growth rate, to increase its stream of returns:

$$ROE = \text{Net profit margin} * \text{Total asset turnover} * \text{Financial leverage}$$

The first two components relate to a firm's operating performance, and together they give a firm's return on assets. Financial leverage relates to the firm's financing decision, and the level of leverage determines the financial risk shareholders will face.

With the factors driving a firm's ROE noted it's possible to estimate a firm's stream of returns. Earlier the growth rate of earnings (g) was defined as the retention rate (RR) multiplied by the return on equity (ROE), g = RR * ROE. And therefore data on the size of a firm's retention rate, net profit margin, total asset turnover, and financial leverage can be used to predict these factors' individual influence, and in turn the growth rate of earnings and an asset's stream of returns. Once this information is used with the investor's required rate of return (examined in the previous section), an investor has the information needed to make an investment decision.

3.4 The Investment Decision

To make sure the required rate of return on an investment will be received, an investor should compare the current market price of the potential investment with their estimation of the investments intrinsic value, before they decide whether or not to invest. If an investor's valuation estimate of the intrinsic value of an investment asset exceeds the current market price of that investment, then they should buy the asset. But if the current market price of an investment exceeds the investor's valuation estimate of the intrinsic value of an investment asset, then the investor should not buy the asset, and should sell it if they already own it:

BUY if:
Estimated Intrinsic Value > Market Price

SELL / DON'T BUY if:
Market Price > Estimated Intrinsic Value

For example, an investor may find that a valuation model values an investment's asset's calculated stream of returns at £50 per share, at the investor's required rate of return. The investor would then compare this £50 estimate of the stock's intrinsic value with the actual publicly available market price, to make a decision on whether or not to invest. If the prevailing market price was lower than £50, at £45 for example, then the investor should decide to buy the investment asset, on the assumption that the asset was currently undervalued and under-priced by the market, and could be expected to rise in value and generate profits for the holder. But if the prevailing market price was greater than the £50 valuation estimate, then the investor should not buy the investment, and would be wise to sell any shares of the asset they currently held. A prevailing market price above the £50 valuation estimate would suggest that the investment was currently overvalued and over-priced by the market, and could be expected to fall in value, causing a loss to anyone who invested in it at the present time, and reduced profits to those who delayed selling it.

The concept of valuation and then investment decision is a simple one, but the methodology used for valuation varies significantly depending on the type of investment asset under consideration. Alternative securities have different characteristics and return streams, and this requires the theory of valuation to be implemented differently in each case. The rest of this book explains a range of popular valuation models, covering both easier to value securities such as bonds and preferred stock, and more difficult to value assets such as common stock. Both the discounted cash flow (DCF) and relative cash flow valuation methods are detailed, each with a range of alternative models to allow for companies' differing circumstances, and varying accessibility to reliable financial information.

4 Bond and Preferred Stock Valuation

4.1 Bond Valuation

The last section noted that the two pieces of information required to value an investment asset are its stream of returns, and the investor's required rate of return. And because the stream of returns associated with a bond is known and certain (assuming the bond issuer doesn't default) the task of valuing a bond is relatively straightforward, with the only unknown being the investor's required rate of return to discount the future stream of returns into their present value.

A bond's stream of returns will typically come in two forms:
(a) Periodic interest payments weighted by the respective share of the annual coupon rate, multiplied by the face value of the bond;
(b) Payment of the principal of the bond on its maturity date.

Periodic interest payments may be annual and see the full annual coupon rate multiplied by the face value of the bond, semi-annual and have half the annual coupon rate multiplied by the face value of the bond, or monthly and see one twelfth of the coupon rate multiplied by the face value of the bond, etc. The principal of the bond paid at maturity is simply the face value of the bond.

Example 1

In 2017 an investor is considering a bond with a £5,000 face value which pays an 8% coupon semi-annually, for 10 years until the bond matures in 2027.

With this information the investment's stream of returns can be determined, assuming the bond issuer does not default, and find themselves out of cash and unable to pay the investor their promised interest and principal payments at the specified time. The investor will receive the £5,000 face value of the bond on maturity after 10 years as a principal payment. And the periodic interest payments will be 4% of the £5,000 face value every six months (i.e. half the 8% annual coupon rate), for 20 periods (i.e. interest payments twice a year for the 10 year life of the bond). 4% of £5,000 equals £200 every six months (0.04 * £5,000 = £200), and therefore there will be 20 interest payments of £200).

The unknown factor is the required rate of return which the investor should use to discount future cash flows into their present value according to the time value of money principle. The prevailing nominal risk-free rate for the investor is 5%, and the investor requires a 3% risk premium to be added to this amount. This is due to there being some probability that the bond issuer may default and be unable to make their interest payments or principal payment on time, due to the risk factors noted earlier in section 3.2. As noted earlier the investor's required rate of return (k) is the sum of the nominal risk-free rate (NRFR) and the investor's risk premium (RP), and therefore the required rate of return is 8%:

$$k = NRFR + RP$$
$$k = 5\% + 3\%$$
$$k = 8\%$$

However, as interest payments occur semi-annually (twice a year), the required rate of return must be divided by two (as it is based around the annual nominal interest rate plus a risk premium). This means that the relevant discount rate in this example is one-half the required rate of return, which is 4%.

With both a stream of returns and the investor's required rate of return the bond valuation process can begin, to turn calculated return values into present values, to account for the time value of money. The 20 periodic interest payments of £200 (twice a year for the 10 year life of the bond) are essentially an annuity, and therefore require a Present Value Interest Factor of an Annuity (PVIFA). The formula for a PVIFA discount factor is as follows, where k is the relevant required rate of return (i.e. one-half the required rate of return for semi-annual interest payments), and N is the number of periods for which interest is paid:

$$PVIFA = [1 - 1/(1 + k)^N] / k$$

Putting the values of k = 0.04 (i.e. 4%), and N = 20 into the above formula gives the equation:

$$PVIFA = [1 - 1/(1 + 0.04)^{20}] / 0.04$$
$$PVIFA = [1 - 0.4563869462] / 0.04$$
$$PVIFA = 13.5903$$

The present value of the 20 semi-annual interest payments of £200, at a 4% discount rate (one-half the required rate of return) is:

$$£200 * 13.5903 = £2,718.06$$

Turning to the principal payment of £5,000 at the end of the bond's 10 year life, this payment is a one-off and therefore requires the standard Present Value Interest Factor (PVIF). The formula for that is as follows, where k is again the relevant required rate of return (so again one-half the required rate of return here), and N is the number of periods for which interest was paid:

$$PVIF = 1/(1 + k)^N$$

Putting the values k = 0.04 and N = 20 into the formula gives the equation:

$$PVIF = 1/(1 + 0.04)^{20}$$
$$PVIF = 0.456387$$

The present value of the principal payment of £5,000 paid at the bond's maturity, discounted at 4% for 20 periods is:

$$£5,000 * 0.456387 = £2,281.94$$

Combining the present value (PV) of the bond's periodic interest payments, with the present value of the bond's principal, gives the total value of a bond at a 8% investor required rate of return:

Total bond value = Present value of interest payments + Present value of principal

$$\text{Total bond value} = £2,718.06 + £2,281.94$$
$$\text{Total bond value} = £5,000$$

The total bond value, which is the maximum that an investor should be willing to pay for a bond, is £5,000 here. If the market price of the bond is any higher than this then the investor should not buy it. At a higher price an investor will not receive their required rate of return, and they will receive a lower yield and a smaller stream of returns than they find acceptable.

Note that the total bond value of £5,000 is exactly equal to the face value of the bond here. When the investor's required rate of return, which determines the bond's value, is equal to the coupon rate, which multiplies by the face value of a bond, this will be the case, as here with both at 8%. But it is worth examining what would happen if an investor's required rate of return was not the same as the coupon rate, and the next example will do that.

Example 2

The bond and economic environment is the same as in example 1, and a 2017 bond with a £5,000 face value and 8% coupon paid semi-annually will hit maturity after 10 years in 2027, while the nominal risk-free rate in the economy is again 5%. However, in this example a different investor is considering the bond and this investor is more risk averse than the one in the previous example. This new investor requires a larger 5% risk premium to calm their nerves and cover the probability that the bond issuer defaults and is unable to make interest payments or principal payment on time. 3% of this (the risk premium in example 1) could be said to be based on a rational calculation of the risks facing the bond issuer, while the remaining 2% of the 5% risk premium could be said to be the investor's irrational panicked overreaction to this risk and uncertainty, due to their heightened level of risk aversion.

An unchanged 8% coupon means the stream of returns is the same as in example 1. The face value of £5,000 will again be received as a principal payment when the bond reaches maturity, and periodic interest payments will again be £200 every six months for 20 periods (i.e. the 8% annual coupon rate divided by two to give a 4% six-monthly rate, multiplied by the bond face value of £5,000).

But a higher 5% risk premium does create a higher required risk of return (k), which is the sum of the nominal risk-free rate of return (NRFR) and the investor's risk premium (RP).

$$k = NRFR + RP$$
$$k = 5\% + 5\%$$
$$k = 10\%$$

But as interest payments are semi-annual and occur twice a year, the required rate of return must again be adjusted to a six-monthly rate by dividing the calculated k value by two. This gives a 5% discount rate with which to turn the stream of returns into present values, to properly value the bond according to the time value of money.

A new discount rate changes the value of the Present Value of Interest Factor for an Annuity (PVIFA), used to turn periodic interest payments into a present value. To calculate it the values of N = 20, and k = 0.05 (i.e. 5%), will be entered into the following PVIFA formula:

$$PVIFA = [1 - 1/(1 + k)^N] / k$$
$$PVIFA = [1 - 1/(1 + 0.05)^{20}] / 0.05$$
$$PVIFA = [1 - 0.3768894829] / 0.05$$
$$PVIFA = 12.4622$$

This discount factor can then be multiplied by the semi-annual interest payment value of £200, to reveal the present value of periodic interest payments at a 5% discount rate:

$$£200 * 12.4622 = £2,492.44$$

Turning next to the principal payment paid at the bond's maturity, this one-off payment is turned to a present value using the standard Present Value of Interest Factor (PVIF) formula, with values of N = 20 and a new discount factor of k = 0.05 (5%):

$$PVIF = 1/(1 + 0.05)^{20}$$
$$PVIF = 0.376889$$

This can then be multiplied by the principal payment of £5,000, to reveal the present value of the principal at a 5% discount rate:

$$£5,000 * 0.376889 = £1,884.45$$

Adding these two present values for interest payments and principal payment together gives the present value of the bond at a 10% investor required rate of return:

Total bond value = Present value of interest payments + Present value of principal

$$\text{Total bond value} = £2,492.44 + £1,884.45$$
$$\text{Total bond value} = £4,376.89$$

The total bond value is £4,376.89 if an investor holds a 10% required rate of return. The investor shouldn't be willing to pay any more than this for the bond, and if the market price is higher the investor should ignore it and look for alternative investments, which can give the yield they require.

Looking at example 1 and example 2 together reveals that the actual value of a bond to an investor falls as their required rate of return rises. Even though the bond itself is unchanged in the two examples, the more risk averse investor in example 2 would pay less money for the bond than the investor in example 1. This shows that an investor that wants a higher return (i.e. has a higher required rate of return), will pay a lower price for a bond asset, and attributes a lower value to a given stream of returns. This makes intuitive sense, as an investor with a higher required rate of return, who demands a greater return from their bond investments, is essentially greedier than other investors. And therefore they will naturally value things less than others, including bond assets, and their stream of returns. Looking at the two examples together also shows the importance of finding the correct values for inputs into a valuation model, and changing the size of just one factor (the investor's risk premium here) makes a big difference to the valuation result.

In example 1 the bond value to the investor was the same as the face value of the bond, but in example 2 the bond value was lower than the face value of the bond. This pattern is directly tied to the relationship between a bond's coupon rate, and the required rate of return of the investor considering the bond. If the coupon rate of a bond is the same as the required rate of return for an investor (as in example 1), then the bond's value to an investor will be exactly the same as the bond's face value. If the coupon rate of a bond is less than the required rate of return of the investor considering the bond (as in example 2), then the value of the bond to the investor will be less than the face value of the bond. And it follows logically, without even having to show it in an example, that if the coupon rate of a bond is greater than an investor's required rate of return, then the value of the bond will be greater to that investor than the face value of a bond.

The noted relationship between a bond's coupon and an investor's required rate of return can allow investors to make investment decisions on bonds, without necessarily having to go through a full valuation process where they calculate the present value of an asset's stream of returns. An investor could simply look at the bond's promised coupon and compare that with their own required rate of return, and then compare the bond's stated face value with its current market price. If the coupon for a bond is less than the investor's required rate of return, implying the bond's value to the investor is less than the bond's face value, then the investor could immediately reject the investment if the prevailing market price matched or exceeded the bond's face value. And if a bond's coupon is greater than the investor's required rate of return, implying that the bond's value to the investor is greater than the bond's face value, then the investor could immediately buy the investment if the prevailing market price matched or was lower than the bond's face value.

4.2 Preferred Stock Valuation

Preferred stock shares several characteristics with bonds, and owners of preferred stock are also promised a periodic dividend payment of a stated amount, to be delivered at specific dates given in advance. But there are two differences between the two types of investment assets. The first difference between bonds and preferred stock is that while bonds offer periodic payments and then a large principal payment at maturity, preferred stock has no maturity and no principal payment, and instead offers periodic payments in perpetuity. A second difference between bonds and preferred stock is that owners of preferred stock have a weaker legal claim to receive what they are promised from the asset issuers than bond holders do. A firm is obligated to pay bond holders before they pay preferred stock holders, and this gives preferred stock holders an increased uncertainty of returns, and a greater risk that the issuer will default and run out of money and be unable to pay preferred stock holders their promised returns on time.

With a greater risk of the issuer defaulting and not meeting their payment obligations, investors should require a higher rate of return on preferred stock than on bonds to make up for it. However, while this may be the case in theory it doesn't necessarily exist in practice in general, as preferred stocks often receive preferential corporate tax rates compared to bonds, and this makes up for the greater risk of the issuer defaulting on payments in the minds of many corporate investors, removing the requirement for a higher rate of return.

As preferred stock is a perpetuity and pays forever, the value of preferred stock can be found by dividing the stock's annual dividend by the investor's required rate of return (k).

$$\text{Preferred stock value} = \text{Annual dividend} / k$$

For example, a preferred stock's annual dividend may be £7 a year, the prevailing nominal risk-free rate of interest may be 5%, and the investor's risk premium may be 5%. The investor's required rate of return equals the nominal risk-free rate plus the investor's risk premium, which is 5% + 5% = 10% (i.e. 0.10). Putting these relevant values into the formula for preferred stock value above gives:

$$\text{Preferred stock value} = \text{Annual dividend} / k$$
$$\text{Preferred stock value} = £7 / 0.10$$
$$\text{Preferred stock value} = £70$$

The value of the preferred stock to this investor is £70, and the investor should pay up to this price for the asset, but no higher. If the market price was higher than £70 then the investor would not receive the 10% required rate of return they require, as a simple example can show. If the market price for the preferred stock was £72 for example, then the rate of return would be:

$$\text{Rate of return} = \text{Dividend} / \text{Market price}$$
$$\text{Rate of return} = £7 / £72$$
$$\text{Rate of return} = 0.0972$$
$$\text{Rate of return} = 9.72\%$$

Any market price above the value of the preferred stock (£70 in this example) will give an unacceptable rate of return below the investor's required rate of return. While any market price below the value of the preferred stock will give a rate of return above that required by the investor.

5 Discounted Cash Flow (DCF) Valuation

5.1 The Basics of DCF Valuation

While the valuation of bonds and preferred stock explained in the last chapter is relatively simple and straightforward, due to an asset's stream of returns being known and certain (unless the issuer defaults on payments), the valuation of common stock is far more complex. Unlike bonds and preferred stock the returns of common stock can change regularly, and with valuation models only ever being as reliable as the inputs put into them, common stock valuation is therefore potentially more unreliable and difficult. Also, common stock holders are paid by asset issuers after both bond holders and preferred stock holders, meaning an increased uncertainty of returns and greater risk that the issuer will default before paying common stock holders, and the promised stream of returns may never materialise.

One way to deal with the problems associated with common stock valuation is to simply operate on the basis that the inputs into the valuation model, the stream of returns and the investor's required rate of return, can be accurately calculated and relied upon despite the difficulties and uncertainty just noted. The Discounted Cash Flow (DCF) valuation approach operates on this basis, and takes an asset's stream of returns, and then uses the investor's required rate of return to discount it into a present value which can be used to make an investment decision. This was done earlier in section 4.1 with bond valuation, and it makes intuitive sense to value investments by determining the present value of cash flows, as this is what investors are ultimately interested in and how people tend to ascribe value.

Due to the fact that common stock has a variable cash flow, unlike bonds examined earlier, the discounting model used to turn future cash flows into present value takes on a different form to that seen earlier. The following model is the basic valuation model used by the discounting cash flow (DCF) valuation approach, and the different types of DCF model which will be examined are all some variation of this basic form:

$$\text{Value of stock} = \sum [CF_t / (1 + k)^t]$$

CF_t is the cash flow associated with the stock in time period t, where t = 1 represents the year 1, t = 2 represents year 2, etc. k is the discount rate which equals the investor's required rate of return for the stock, which is the sum of the nominal interest rate and the investor's risk premium, and this risk premium is determined by the level of uncertainty associated with the stock's cash flows. Finally, $\sum$ represents the summation of all discounted cash flows for all time periods under consideration, i.e. the present value of year one's cash flows, plus the present value of year two's cash flows, the present value of year three's cash flows etc.

While all discounted cash flow techniques are based around this basic model, they disagree on how the cash flow stream of returns associated with a firm's stock should be represented in the valuation model, and on the investor's discount rate. Three alternative discounted cash flow methods and the basic differences between them are summarized in the following paragraphs.

The Dividend Discount Model (DDM) measures cash flow using dividends, which makes intuitive sense as dividends are the cash flows which go directly to the investor. As the DDM focuses on the cash flows which go directly to shareholders the discount rate does the same, using the cost of equity as the discount rate, which is the shareholder's required rate of return on an equity investment (i.e. k, as explained earlier). The DDM model is most useful for stock valuation of a stable mature firm where relatively constant growth is assumed over the long-term. However the DDM's dividend focussed approach is difficult to apply to those firms which invest internally and don't pay dividends during periods of high growth, or which pay very small dividends due to alternative investment opportunities offering a high rate of return.

As the name suggests the Present Value of Operating Free Cash Flow model represents cash flow with the operating free cash flow measure. This is usually defined as cash flows after direct costs, (i.e. cost of goods, plus selling, general and administrative expenses), working capital outlays, and capital expenditures for future growth, but before accounting for payments to capital suppliers. In accounting terms operating free cash flow is net income after amortization and depreciation, after recording the change in working capital, but before adjusting for payments to debt holders. The term 'free' is used in the description as it refers to cash flow which is free to be used, after the firm's asset base has been maintained with other funds. As the operating free cash flow measure of cash flow examines the cash flows for all capital suppliers and not just shareholders, it involves both equity and debt. As a result the discount rate used to turn operating free cash flow into a present value must also incorporate both equity and debt, and therefore the firm's weighted average cost of capital (WACC) is used as the discount rate, and this weights the costs of debt and equity by the weight of debt and equity in the firm's value. The present value of operating free cash flow model is useful if an investor seeks to compare stocks from firms with diverse capital structures, as investors can determine the value of the total firm and then subtract the value of a firm's debt, to reveal the value of each firm's equity.

Taking operating free cash flow as explained above, and then subtracting payments to debt holders (i.e. capital expenditures) gives the free cash flow to equity. And this is the cash flow measure used in the Present Value of Free Cash Flow to Equity model. As this model represents cash flow after a firm's debt is paid off and gone cash flow is entirely based on equity, and therefore the discount rate used by the model is the cost of equity. The present value of free cash flow to equity model would be the most appropriate to use if there was a difficulty using a dividend model, for reasons just noted, or if firms had no debt.

All of the three present value of cash flows models summarized can either be used to estimate a stock's cash flow for an individual year, or cash flow over an extended period to allow a general prediction for the stock's overall growth rate. However, the discounted cash flow models are all highly dependent on the values of two inputs, and as suggested earlier they assume that the estimates of the growth rate (both the level and duration) of cash flows, and the discount rate, are accurate. If the two estimates of these inputs are even slightly off then the discounted cash flow valuation models may be misleading, but if they are accurate then the valuation models should be both efficient and superior to alternatives.

5.2 Dividend Discount Model (DDM)

The Dividend Discount Model (DDM) operates on the assumption that the value of a firm's common stock equals the present value of all of the stock's future dividends. The DDM formula for valuing common stock is therefore as follows, where k is the required rate of return, D_1 represents the stock's dividend in year 1, D_2 is the stock's dividend in year 2, etc.:

$$\text{Value of stock} = [D_1 / (1 + k)^1] + [D_2 / (1 + k)^2] + \ldots + [D_\infty / (1 + k)^\infty]$$

This can be shortened to make an easier formula, where $\sum$ represents the sum of present values, and t represents year 1 if t = 1, t represents year 2 if t = 2 etc.

$$\text{Value of stock} = \sum [D_t / (1 + k)^t]$$

In the former of these two formulas the time period for receiving dividends extended to period ∞, infinity, suggesting that the investor would receive dividends for the entire life of the stock. However, in practice the investor will not hold the stock for its entire life, but will instead hold it for a limited period of time and then sell it on to someone else. Therefore a new version of the DDM formula is required to take into account the selling of the stock at some point in the future. If an investor was to buy common stock and then sell it at the end of two years, then they would receive year one's dividends, year two's dividends, and the selling price of the asset at the end of year two, all of which would need to be discounted to turn them into present values. The dividend discount model equation for the value of the stock would be as follows, where SP_2 is the selling price (SP) of the asset at the end of year two ($_2$):

Stock value = $[D_1/(1 + k)^1] + [D_2/(1 + k)^2] + [SP_2/(1 + k)^2]$

As the dividend discount model says that the value of a stock is the sum of the present values of all of its future dividends, the value of the stock when it is sold after two years will be the sum of the present values of the dividend in year 3, year 4, year 5 etc. for all future periods. And with the assumption of an efficient market, where the price of a good equals its value, the selling price of the stock after two years, SP_2, will also equal the sum of the present values of all of its future dividends. The dividend to be received in three years, D_3, will be the next period's dividend by the time the stock is sold after two years, and SP_2 will at that point be the present. Therefore instead of being turned into a present value (present in terms of SP_2, when the stock is sold after two years), by being divided by $(1 + k)^3$, the dividend D_3 will only need to be divided by $(1 + k)$ to be turned into a present value. And accordingly the following year's dividend D_4 would be turned into a present value by being divided by $(1 + k)^2$, etc. Therefore the value or selling price of the stock after two years, SP_2, will equal the following formula:

$$SP_2 = [D_3/(1 + k)] + [D_4/(1 + k)^2] + \ldots + [D_\infty/(1 + k)^\infty]$$

The value of SP_2 has now been found, but in the full formula for the stock value earlier there was not a SP_2 term, but a $SP_2 / (1 + k)^2$ term. Therefore the formula for SP_2 just determined should be divided by $(1 + k)^2$ to turn it into a $SP_2 / (1 + k)^2$ formula, in preparation for putting it back into the formula for stock value when stock is sold after two years:

$$SP_2/(1+k)^2 = \{[D_3/(1+k)] + [D_4/(1+k)^2] + \ldots + [D_\infty/(1+k)^\infty]\} / (1 + k)^2$$
$$SP_2/(1+k)^2 = [D_3/(1+k)^3] + [D_4/(1+k)^4] + \ldots + [D_\infty/(1+k)^\infty]$$

Putting this term into the stock value formula when stock is sold after two years gives:

Stock value $= [D_1/(1 + k)^1] + [D_2/(1 + k)^2] + [SP_2/(1 + k)^2]$
Stock value $= [D_1/(1 + k)^1] + [D_2/(1 + k)^2] + [D_3/(1+k)^3] + [D_4/(1+k)^4] + \ldots + [D_\infty/(1+k)^\infty]$

This result reveals that the stock value when a stock is sold after two years is equal to the stock value when a stock is not sold. And this stock value equals the sum of the present values of all future dividends, as the dividend discount model predicts a stock's value will always be.

One obvious criticism of the dividend discount model's method of using future dividends to value a stock is the existence of stocks which do not pay dividends. But such criticism doesn't hold up in practice. The dividend discount model would simply model a non-dividend paying stock as having zero dividends in the foreseeable near future (e.g. $D_1 = 0$, $D_2 = 0$), but expected to pay dividend payments longer into the future. If investors actually thought a stock would never ever pay dividends then they wouldn't be willing to purchase the stock, as it has no value, and it wouldn't be feasible as a security. In practice a firm which doesn't currently pay dividends on its stock is likely to have decided that its capital is better off being reinvested, suggesting that the firm has access to very profitable projects which will generate larger and faster growing earnings and dividend streams in the future.

With the theory behind the dividend discount model explained, the next step is to look at an example to see how it works in practice. And while it is easy for the DDM to state that a stock's value will be the value of all of its future dividends, actually calculating what these far off future dividends will be worth must rely on estimation.

Example

An investor intends to buy a stock, hold it for two years and then sell it, and needs to determine the stock's value to decide how much he should be willing to pay for it. The firm whose stock is under consideration earned £2 per share last year, and paid a dividend of £0.60 per share. This represented a 30% payout ratio, and the firm has been consistent in paying out approximately this rate over a prolonged period. Analysis suggests that the firm's earnings will grow approximately 5% per year for the next two years. The current yield on 10 year government bonds is 4%. Finally, the investor considering the stock requires a 3% risk premium on any risky investment, to make up for the potential uncertainty of the cash flows.

With this information the coming year's expected dividend, D_1, can be found for the stock. Current earnings of £2 per share are forecast to increase 5% over the next year, and £2 * 1.05 = £2.10 earnings per share for year 1. With the firm's dividend payout ratio expected to be stable at about 30%, the dividend per share for year 1, D_1, will be £2.10 * 0.3 = £0.63. This dividend for the next year represents a 5% increase from the last year's dividend of £0.60, and with a constant payout ratio a 5% increase in earnings in a year corresponds to a 5% increase in dividends in a year. As a reliable 5% earnings growth rate is expected for the second year too, year two's earnings are estimated at 5% greater than year one's, which was just calculated at £2.10 per share. £2.10 * 1.05 = £2.205 or £2.21 earnings per share for year two. As a 30% payout ratio has been relatively consistently paid out by the firm it can be assumed again for year two, which means D_2 dividends are £2.21 * 0.30 = £0.663 or £0.66. This is again a 5% dividend growth rate for year two.

A 10 year yield on government bonds at 4% represents the nominal risk-free rate of interest (NRFR), which can be added to the 3% risk premium (RP) of the investor to reveal their required rate of return (k). k = NRFR + RP, k = 4% + 3% = 7%. Therefore the investor's required rate of return for this investment is 7%.

Now that estimated values have been calculated for dividends for the coming year, D_1 = £0.63, dividends in two years, D_2 = £0.66, and the investor's required rate of return, k = 7% or 0.07, the stock valuation process can begin. Earlier the formula for an investor who planned to buy a stock, hold it for two years, and then sell it, was revealed to be the discounted values of the two years dividends and the selling price in year 2:

Stock value = $[D_1/(1 + k)^1] + [D_2/(1 + k)^2] + [SP_2/(1 + k)^2]$

Using values for D_1, D_2, and k, the first two terms making up the stock value, $[D_1/(1 + k)^1] + [D_2/(1 + k)^2]$, can be calculated.

$$[D_1/(1+k)^1] = 0.63 / (1 + 0.07)$$
$$[D_1/(1+k)^1] = 0.63 / (1.07)$$
$$[D_1/(1+k)^1] = £0.59$$

$$[D_2/(1+k)^2] = 0.66 / (1 + 0.07)^2$$
$$[D_2/(1+k)^2] = 0.66 / (1.07)^2$$
$$[D_2/(1+k)^2] = 0.66 / 1.1449$$
$$[D_2/(1+k)^2] = £0.58$$

Combining these two calculated numbers gives the present value of dividends for the two years the investor is planning to hold the stock, and £0.58 + £0.59 = £1.17 in dividends. This just leaves the final term in the stock value formula, $[SP_2/(1+k)^2]$ to be calculated. The value of k is already known but the selling price after two years, SP_2, is unknown and must be found. There are three methods to find the selling price and each will be examined in turn.

The first method to estimate the selling price uses the earnings multiplier model, and multiplies expected future earnings by an estimated earnings multiple, to create an expected selling price for the stock. This earnings multiplier is also known as a price-to-earnings (P/E) ratio, and the idea is that the latest available year's earnings value is multiplied by the expected long-run price-to-earnings ratio, to generate a stock selling price which represents the stock's long-run expected earnings. The process used to find this P/E ratio will be explained in depth in section 6.2, but for the example here an estimate will be used. The long-run P/E ratio for stocks is roughly 14, which means that prices are 14 times earnings. The last earnings value estimated before the stock is to be sold after two years was year two's expected earnings, which was found to be £2.21 per share. Multiplying these two numbers together will reveal the estimated stock selling price, SP_2, according to the earnings multiplier model:

$$SP_2 = \text{Year 2 earnings} * \text{Expected long-run P/E}$$
$$SP_2 = £2.21 * 14$$
$$SP_2 = £30.94$$

This value then must be turned from cash flow to be received two years in the future into a present value:

$$[SP_2/(1 + k)^2] = 30.94 / 1.07^2$$
$$[SP_2/(1 + k)^2] = £27.02$$

With this final piece of information the value of the stock can be found, according to the earnings multiplier model. The investor should pay £28.19 at most for the stock, or they won't receive their required rate of return:

$$\text{Stock value} = [D_1/(1 + k)^1] + [D_2/(1 + k)^2] + [SP_2/(1 + k)^2]$$
$$\text{Stock value} = £0.58 + £0.59 + £27.02$$
$$\text{Stock value} = £28.19$$

The second method to estimate the selling price of a stock is the dividend yield method. This divides a stock's dividends by the expected long-run dividend yield, which is the percentage of a stock's share price that is paid out as dividends, to estimate the stock's price using expected long-run dividends. The average long-run yield on stocks has been somewhere between 1% and 5%, and the 3% (i.e. 0.03) middle point between these two can be used as an estimate for the stock here, due to an absence of further information. The last dividends value calculated before the stock is to be sold at the end of two years was D_2, the dividend for year two, which was estimated at £0.66. Dividing this dividend value by the estimated dividend yield gives an estimated stock selling price, SP_2, as follows:

SP_2 = Year 2 dividend / Expected long-run dividend yield
SP_2 = £0.66 / 0.03
SP_2 = £22

As before this value must then be turned from cash flow to be received two years in the future into a present value:

$$[SP_2/(1 + k)^2] = 22 / 1.07^2$$
$$[SP_2/(1 + k)^2] = £19.22$$

Using the discounted value for the selling price of the stock after two years the overall value of the stock can now be found, according to the dividend yield method of valuation. This reveals that the investor should pay no more than £20.39 for one share of the stock, to ensure they receive at least their required 7% rate of return:

$$\text{Stock value} = [D_1/(1 + k)^1] + [D_2/(1 + k)^2] + [SP_2/(1 + k)^2]$$
$$\text{Stock value} = £0.58 + £0.59 + £19.22$$
$$\text{Stock value} = £20.39$$

The third and final method used to estimate the selling price of a stock is a special type of the dividend discount model (DDM) explained in this section.

Infinite Period Dividend Discount Model

Just as every stock's value equals the value of future dividends under the dividend discount model, earlier in this section it was found that the selling price of a stock held for two years equals the value of all future dividends:

$$SP_2 = [D_3/(1 + k)] + [D_4/(1 + k)^2] + \ldots + [D_\infty/(1 + k)^\infty]$$

Therefore the task to find the selling price of the stock after two years, SP_2, can simply be seen as calculating the value of all future dividends from year 3 onwards to infinity. As this is clearly a very difficult task the last two methods of finding a stock's selling price avoided it, as the earnings multiplier model instead estimated a relationship between predicted earnings and a future stock price, while the dividend yield model estimated a relationship between predicted dividends and a future stock price. But the apparent herculean task of predicting all of a stock's future dividends from now until the end of time can be made feasible, with a simplifying assumption that the stream of future dividends will grow at a constant rate for infinity.

The infinite period dividend discount model (DDM), also known as the Gordon Growth Model, estimates the value of a stock with two assumptions: the dividend growth rate is constant, and remains constant forever. This changes the formula of the DDM from the original form:

$$\text{Value of stock} = [D_1 / (1 + k)^1] + [D_2 / (1 + k)^2] + \ldots + [D_\infty / (1 + k)^\infty]$$

And the new form of the DDM is as follows, where g is the constant growth rate of dividends, k is the investor's required rate of return, and D_1 is next year's dividend:

$$\text{Value of stock} = D_1 / (k - g)$$

This formula reveals the third (implicit) assumption of the Gordon growth model, that the required rate of return exceeds the constant growth rate. If this is not the case then the denominator will be negative and the model gives useless results. Therefore the constant growth model cannot be used to forecast the present value of long-run dividends until the estimated growth rate is predicted to have fallen below the required rate of return, and dividends must be discounted year by year until that point.

As the stock to be valued in this example is the selling price of a stock two years from now, the relevant next period's dividend in the model would be the dividend for year 3, which is the next period after the stock is sold. Therefore, looking at it from the present day, the formula to determine the value of the stock and a suitable selling price after two years when it is to be sold, SP_2, is:

$$SP_2 = D_3 / (k - g)$$

Earlier on the investor's required return was calculated at $k = 7\%$ (0.07), and the dividend growth rate for the first two years was noted to be 5%. A constant growth rate forever is assumed but the specific rate must be estimated, and the most appropriate rate to use would be that already calculated for years one and two, at $g = 5\%$ (i.e. 0.05) per year. That just leaves the value of D_3, the dividend for year 3, the first year after the stock is sold. With a dividend growth rate of 5% every year predicted, this will simply be 5% greater than the value of the second year's dividend,

D_2, which was earlier estimated to be at £0.66. $D_3 = 1.05 * 0.66 = £0.69$. With values for all parts of the selling price formula above now accumulated, a value for selling price SP_2 can be found according to the infinite period dividend discount model:

$$SP_2 = D_3 / (k - g)$$
$$SP_2 = 0.69 / (0.07 - 0.05)$$
$$SP_2 = £34.50$$

Like the other two methods of calculating a stock selling price this SP_2 value must be turned into a present value, to account for the time value of money, by dividing it by the applicable discount rate:

$$[SP_2/(1 + k)^2] = 34.50 / 1.07^2$$
$$[SP_2/(1 + k)^2] = £30.13$$

And this can be added to the present values of the dividends for year 1 and year 2 found earlier, to give the total value of the stock in this example according to the infinite period dividend discount model:

$$\text{Stock value} = [D_1/(1 + k)^1] + [D_2/(1 + k)^2] + [SP_2/(1 + k)^2]$$
$$\text{Stock value} = £0.58 + £0.59 + £30.13$$
$$\text{Stock value} = £31.30$$

The infinite DDM values the stock at £31.30 and suggests that the investor can afford to pay as much as this for the stock and still receive their required rate of return. This is a higher valuation than the earnings multiplier model which suggested the investor should pay no more than £28.19, while the dividend yield method suggested an even lower stock value to the investor of £20.39. The difference between these three valuations highlights the significance of what is put into a model, and bad erroneous inputs into a valuation model will create a bad erroneous valuation, while good accurate inputs into a model will ensure a good accurate valuation. Changing the estimated long-run P/E ratio would completely change the earnings multiplier model valuation, changing the estimated long-run dividend yield would radically change that model's valuation, and even a small change in the constant growth rate or required rate of return would ensure a very different valuation by the infinite period dividend discount model.

While the infinite period DDM has generated a stock valuation which could be plausible in this example, in reality the assumptions of the infinite period dividend discount model are unlikely to hold for every firm's stock. Empirical evidence shows that some firms (growth firms) will not have constant dividend growth for eternity, but may instead go through temporary periods with very high growth in earnings and dividend payout, causing the growth rate of dividends to exceed an investor's required rate of return for a period of time. As the infinite period dividend discount model does not allow for non-constant dividend growth, or for the growth rate of dividends to exceed an investor's required rate of return, a modified version of the DDM is required to represent this scenario.

Supernormal Growth Dividend Discount Model

The infinite period dividend discount model just examined allowed for all future dividends to be valued, as one dividend growth rate was used for the entire duration of a stock's life. And the original dividend discount model examined at the start of this section allowed for any chosen dividend growth rate to be used, as each year's dividend was calculated separately. In order to value the stocks of firms which will go through temporary periods of supernormal growth in earnings and dividends payouts, the two dividend discount models must be combined. This means the entire future dividend stream for a firm's stock will be valued, but periods with different rates of growth will be valued separately.

An example can explain how the supernormal growth dividend discount model operates. A firm has a current dividend (D_0) of £1.80, and the dividend growth rate is expected to grow 20% per year for the next two years, then 15% per year for years three and four after that, before the dividend growth rate stabilises off at 10% for year five onwards. The company's cost of equity is 12%. The nominal interest rate is 7%, and the rate of inflation is 2%.

Growth rates for years 1-4 and then the constant growth rate from year 5 onwards is supplied in the above information which allows for the respective dividend streams to be found. The only other factor required to use the supernormal growth dividend discount model is the required rate of return, and the 12% cost of equity is the relevant rate to use as returns come in the form of a firm's dividends. The extra information supplied, on the nominal rate of interest and the rate of inflation, is not needed to find the required rate of return here, and can be ignored. Based on the fact that there will be four years of non-constant growth rates, then a constant growth rate from year five to infinity, the formula for the stock's value is:

$$\text{Stock value} = [D_1/(1 + k)] + [D_2/(1 + k)^2] + [D_3/(1 + k)^3] + [D_4/(1 + k)^4] + \{[D_5/(k - g)] / (1 + k)^5\}$$

The terms $[D_1/(1 + k)^1]$, $[D_2/(1 + k)^2]$ etc. represent the present value of the first year dividend, the present value of the second year dividend etc. as used earlier. And the $[D_5/(k - g)]$ term is the constant dividend from year five onwards, while $(1 + k)^5$ turns this constant dividend from year five onwards into a present value. With the formula explained numerical values can now be entered into it, to determine the example stock's value according to the supernormal growth dividend discount model. The information supplied at the start of this subsection revealed that D_0, the current dividend, equals £1.80. $D_1 = 1.80*1.20 = £2.16$, as the D_1 dividend next year will be 20% higher (i.e. *1.20) than D_0. D_2 is estimated to be 20% higher still (i.e. *1.20 again), and therefore $D_2 = 2.16*1.20 = £2.59$. The dividend for year three D_3 is forecast to be 15% higher than the last year (i.e. *1.15), and so $D_3 = 2.59*1.15 = £2.98$. Year four's dividend is 15% higher again, $D_4 = £2.98*1.15 = £3.43$. And the constant dividend rate for year five onwards is 10% higher than D_4, and therefore $D_5 = 3.43*1.10 = £3.77$. The cost of equity is the required rate of return, $k = 0.12$ (i.e. 12%), and the constant growth rate from year five onwards is 10%, $g = 0.10$. Putting all of this data into the stock value formula gives:

Stock value = $[D_1/(1 + k)] + [D_2/(1 + k)^2] + [D_3/(1 + k)^3] + [D_4/(1 + k)^4] + \{[D_5/(k - g)] / (1 + k)^5\}$

Stock value = $[2.16/1.12] + [2.59/(1.12)^2] + [2.98/(1.12)^3] + [3.43/(1.12)^4] + \{[3.77/(0.12 - 0.10)] / (1.12)^5\}$

Stock value = £1.93 + £2.06 + £2.12 + £2.18 + £106.96
Stock value = £115.25

Based on predicted future dividend cash flows, the present value of the stock is estimated at £115.25. The investor should pay no more than this, as the stock is worth only £115.25 to the investor and paying more would see them receive a rate of return lower than their required rate of return of 12%.

This is the end of the discussion on different dividend discount model methods, and the next two sections examine alternative measures of cash flow and discount rate, while maintaining the discounted cash flow method of valuing stocks.

5.3 Present Value of Operating Free Cash Flow

At times measuring cash flow using dividends may not be appropriate, as dividends may not be a good representation of the earnings associated with a stock or firm. An alternative measure of a firm's cash flow is Operating Free Cash Flow (OFCF), and as explained in section 5.1, this is cash flow after all direct costs have been accounted for, including capital expenditures to maintain the firm's asset bases, but before payments to debt holders are deducted.

Operating Free Cash Flow, OFCF =
EBIT*(1 − Tax rate) + (Depreciation + Amortization) − (Change in net working capital) − (Capital expenditures)

Where EBIT is a firm's earnings before interest and taxes. As debt payments have not yet been subtracted the OFCF measure involves both debt and equity, and therefore the discount rate used to turn estimated future cash flows into present values must also include both debt and equity. The discount rate used is therefore the weighted average cost of capital (WACC), and this weights the costs of debt and equity by the weight of debt and equity in the firm's value respectively. The formula for the WACC is as follows:

$$WACC = w_E * k_E + w_D * k_D * (1 - \text{Tax rate})$$

Where w_E is the proportion or weight of equity in the total capital of the firm, which equals the value of a firm's equity, divided by the sum of the value of the firm's equity and the value of the firm's debt. k_E is the cost of equity. w_D is the proportion or weight of debt in the total capital of the firm, which equals the value of a firm's debt, divided by the sum of the value of the firm's equity and the value of the firm's debt. k_D is the cost of debt, determined by the interest rate. As a firm must also pay tax on its debt the debt rate portion of the above formula must account for the tax rate, and it is therefore multiplied by (1 – Tax rate). The weights in the WACC formula can be based on relative book values of debt and equity, or on relative market values, or the middle ground of the two can be used.

With formulas for the operating free cash flow (OFCF), and the weighted average cost of capital (WACC) to use as a discount rate, it is possible to use the Present Value of Operating Free Cash Flow discounted cash flow method to find the value of a firm. Once the method has found a value for the total firm the value of a firm's debt can be subtracted, to reveal the value of a firm's equity (i.e. stock). The formula for the present value of OFCF is the same as the last section with the dividend discount model, except OFCF replaces dividend cash flow, and the

WACC replaces the investor's required rate of return on equity k:

$$\text{Value of firm} = \sum [OFCF_t / (1 + WACC)^t]$$

And if a firm had constant growth then the formula would follow the same constant growth model as put forward in the last section:

$$\text{Value of firm} = OFCF_1 / (WACC - g_{OFCF})$$

Where $OFCF_1$ is the operating free cash flow for year one, equal to the last year's OFCF plus the growth rate in operating free cash flow, $OFCF_1 = OFCF_0(1 + g_{OFCF})$.

An estimate of the long-run growth rate of OFCF, g_{OFCF}, can be found using the formula that follows:

$$g_{OFCF} = RR * ROIC$$

Where RR is the firm's average Retention Rate, the percentage of income retained to grow the firm instead of being paid out as dividends, where RR = 1 – Payout ratio. ROIC is the Return on Invested Capital, where ROIC = [EBIT*(1 – Tax rate)] / Total capital.

The Present Value of Operating Free Cash Flow method can be explained best with an example.

Example

A firm's operating free cash flow for the last year was £2 million. The firm's recent payout ratio is roughly 20%, and the firm has 1,000,000 shares. Its EBIT is £16 million, and the tax rate for the firm is 20%. The firm's total capital is £150 million, which a firm's books states is made up from £120 million equity assets, and £30 million in debt payments, a 80:20 ratio in favour of equity. However, the market values the firm's assets differently at a 90:10 equity to debt ratio in favour of equity. The firm's cost of equity is 12%, and the interest rate is 5%.

There is a lot of information here and the best place to start is to try and find what is required for the value of a firm formula. The value of a firm according to the operating free cash flow discounting method has been stated as: Value of firm = $OFCF_1 / (WACC - g_{OFCF})$. And the three parts of this formula can be found using the three additional formulas: $OFCF_1 = OFCF_0(1 + g_{OFCF})$, WACC = $w_E*k_E + w_D*k_D*(1 - \text{Tax rate})$, g_{OFCF} = RR*ROIC. The growth rate of OFCF, g_{OFCF}, is a good place to start and this requires calculating the retention rate (RR) and the return on invested capital (ROIC):

$$RR = 1 - \text{Payout ratio}$$
$$RR = 1 - 0.2$$
$$RR = 0.8$$

$$\text{ROIC} = [\text{EBIT}*(1 - \text{Tax rate})] / \text{Total capital.}$$
$$\text{ROIC} = [16{,}000{,}000*(1 - 0.2)] / 150{,}000{,}000$$
$$\text{ROIC} = 12{,}800{,}000 / 150{,}000{,}000$$
$$\text{ROIC} = 0.0853$$

Putting RR = 0.8 and ROIC = 0.0853 into the OFCF growth formula gives:

$$g_{OFCF} = 0.8*0.0853$$
$$g_{OFCF} = 0.06824$$
$$g_{OFCF} = 6.824\%$$

To simplify matters 6.824% will be rounded to 7%, and therefore the growth of operating free cash flow is 7%. With no information to the contrary this will be assumed to be a constant growth rate. The next step is to find the weighted average cost of capital (WACC). This will be done using both book value weights and market value weights, as the average of the two is used to balance any discrepancy between the firm's book valuation and the market valuation. The book WACC weights are:

$$\text{Weight of debt, } w_D = 30{,}000{,}000/150{,}000{,}000$$
$$\text{Weight of debt, } w_D = 0.20$$

$$\text{Weight of equity, } w_E = 120{,}000{,}000/150{,}000{,}000$$
$$\text{Weight of equity, } w_E = 0.80$$

And with the cost of equity (k_E) at 12%, and the interest rate for debt (k_D) at 5%, the book value WACC, $WACC_B$ is:

$$WACC = w_E * k_E + w_D * k_D * (1 - \text{Tax rate})$$
$$WACC_B = 0.8 * 0.12 + 0.2 * 0.05 * (1 - 0.2)$$
$$WACC_B = 0.096 + 0.008$$
$$WACC_B = 0.104$$
$$WACC_B = 10.4\%$$

The market WACC weights are:

$$\text{Weight of debt, } w_D = 0.10$$
$$\text{Weight of equity, } w_E = 0.90$$

And with these weights, the costs of equity and debt, and the tax rate, the market value WACC, $WACC_M$ is:

$$WACC = w_E * k_E + w_D * k_D * (1 - \text{Tax rate})$$
$$WACC_M = 0.9 * 0.12 + 0.1 * 0.05 * (1 - 0.2)$$
$$WACC_M = 0.108 + 0.004$$
$$WACC_M = 0.112$$
$$WACC_M = 11.2\%$$

The weighted average cost of capital using the firm's book value of debt and equity weights, $WACC_B$, is 10.4%. And the weighted average cost of capital using the market value weights, $WACC_M$, is 11.2%. Without any information on which of these two is likely to be closer to the truth the average of the two will be used, which gives a weighted average cost of capital at WACC = 10.8%, which will be rounded to 11%. Fortunately, this WACC value is higher than the growth rate estimated earlier at 7%, and this means that the constant growth formula, Value of firm = $OFCF_1$ / (WACC − g_{OFCF}), can be used. If the WACC required rate of return had been estimated to be lower than the forecasted growth rate then the present value of each year's cash flow would have to be calculated year by year, using the same method as in the last section with dividends, using the formula:

$$\text{Year t OFCF} = OFCF_t / (1 + WACC)^t$$

But that isn't the case here, and therefore the firm can be valued using the constant growth formula. First, the value of $OFCF_1$ needs to be found, where $OFCF_0$ is the value of last year's operating free cash flow:

$$OFCF_1 = OFCF_0(1 + g_{OFCF})$$
$$OFCF_1 = 2{,}000{,}000(1 + 0.07)$$
$$OFCF_1 = £2{,}140{,}000$$

And with $OFCF_1$ the present value of the firm can be found according to the operating free cash flow method:

$$\text{Value of firm} = \text{OFCF}_1 / (\text{WACC} - g_{\text{OFCF}})$$
$$\text{Value of firm} = 2{,}140{,}000 / (0.11 - 0.07)$$
$$\text{Value of firm} = 2{,}140{,}000 / (0.04)$$
$$\text{Value of firm} = £53{,}500{,}000$$

The value of the firm is found to be £53,500,000. But an investor will not be interested in the total value of the firm including debt and equity, only the equity of the firm and the value of its stock. And therefore the value of the debt must be subtracted. The firm's book value of debt is £30,000,000, and with 1,000,000 shares the value of equity per share is:

$$\text{Value of equity per share} =$$
$$(\text{Total firm value} - \text{Book debt value}) / \text{Number of shares}$$

$$\text{Value of equity per share} =$$
$$(£53{,}500{,}000 - £30{,}000{,}000) / 1{,}000{,}000$$

$$\text{Book value of equity per share} = £23.50$$

This result suggests that an investor should only pay £23.50 at most for an equity share of the firm's stock. If the current market price is lower the investor should buy the stock, but if the market price is higher the investor should look elsewhere for an investment.

5.4 Present Value of Free Cash Flow to Equity

Another measure of cash flow is Free Cash Flow to Equity (FCFE), and this measure can be calculated by taking the Operating Free Cash Flow measure and then subtracting payments to debt holders. Specifically free cash flow to equity equals:

Free Cash Flow to Equity, FCFE =
(Net income) + (Depreciation + Amortization) − (Change in net working capital) − (Capex) + (Net borrowing)

This formula differs from the operating free cash flow measure in two ways. First, net income replaces the EBIT*(1 − Tax rate) term, as the interest and tax on debt has been subtracted. Second, a net borrowing term has been added to the end of the formula to represent the level of debt, and this will be a negative term to be subtracted if the firm has debt.

With debt subtracted from cash flow and only equity being represented, the relevant discount rate will be the cost of equity (k), as the name free cash flow to equity would suggest. The formula for a stock's value is therefore the same as for the dividend discount model examined earlier, except a year's dividend is replaced with that year's free cash flow to equity (FCFE$_t$). With different growth rates in the FCFE the relevant formula for a stock's value is:

$$\text{Value of stock} = \sum [\text{FCFE}_t / (1 + k)^t]$$

And with constant growth the formula is:

$$\text{Value of stock} = \text{FCFE}_1 / (k - g_{\text{FCFE}})$$

Example

A firm's free cash flow to equity for the year just gone was £350,000. The firm has 2,500,000 shares issued. The firm's cost of equity is 8%. The current growth rate for the firm has been a stable 10% per year, but its market is forecast to begin a period of transition which will see the firm's growth rate fall to 9% three years from now, then to 8% the year after, and 7% the year after that. The firm's long-run growth rate is estimated to be stable at 7% from that period onwards.

The information above for the firm's stock growth rate suggests a three-stage growth model. First, growth in free cash flow to equity, g$_{\text{FCFE}}$, is constant at 10% a year for years one and two. The second stage sees growth fall by 1% a year, as year three's growth falls to 9%, year four's declines to 8%, and year five's growth slows to 7%. And the third stage in the growth model sees constant growth at 7% from that period onwards. The first four years of growth are not lower than the cost of equity required rate of return and therefore the constant growth model cannot be used for this period, and present values must be calculated individually. But from year five on the growth rate is lower than the cost of equity required rate of return, and is constant at 7%, and therefore the constant growth rate can be used.

In terms of the values to put into the Present Value of Free Cash Flow to Equity (FCFE) stock value formula, current FCFE is £350,000, $FCFE_0$ = £350,000. One year from now this is forecast to be 10% higher, $FCFE_1$ = £350,000*1.10 = £385,000. Year two's free cash flow to equity growth will see this 10% higher again, $FCFE_2$ = £385,000*1.10 = £423,500. Year three's FCFE is estimated at 9% greater, $FCFE_3$ = £423,500*1.09 = £461,615. Year four's FCFE is forecast for an 8% increase, $FCFE_4$ = £461,615*1.08 = £498,544.20. And year five's growth rate is 7%, $FCFE_5$ = £498,544.20*1.07 = £533,442.29. This gives the following formula for the stock's value:

$$\text{Stock value} = [FCFE_1/(1 + k)] + [FCFE_2/(1 + k)^2] + [FCFE_3/(1 + k)^3] + [FCFE_4/(1 + k)^4] + \{[FCFE_5/(k - g_{FCFE})] / (1 + k)^5\}$$

$$\text{Stock value} = [385{,}000/(1.08)] + [423{,}500/(1.08)^2] + [461{,}615/(1.08)^3] + [498{,}544.20/(1.08)^4] + [533{,}442.29/(0.08 - 0.07)]/(1.08)^5$$

$$\text{Stock value} = £356{,}481.48 + £363{,}082.99 + £366{,}444.87 + £366{,}444.87 + £36{,}305{,}185.92$$

$$\text{Stock value} = £37{,}757{,}640.13$$

$$\text{Stock value per share} = £37{,}757{,}640.13 / 2{,}500{,}000$$
$$\text{Stock value per share} = £15.10$$

The stock's value per share is £15.10 according to the present value of free cash flow to equity method. An investor should pay this amount or less for one share of the stock, and paying any more is not worth the investment.

6 Relative Valuation Models

6.1 The Basics of Relative Valuation

The last chapter examined the various different types of discounted cash flow techniques, where a stock is valued by estimating future cash flows, which are then discounted into present values using an appropriate discount rate. However, the valuations of all discounted cash flow methods are completely dependent on the accuracy of the cash flow and discount rate inputs used in them, and a slight deviation in input values can transform the valuation. This makes it very important for an investor to update their inputs as the prevailing environment changes.

Relative valuation methods are designed to give an investor greater insight into the wider environment, by providing information on how the aggregate market, alternative industries, and individual stocks within an industry are performing. While the discounted cash flow valuation techniques focus on company analysis, examining a company's cash flow and cost of equity, relative valuation focuses on economy analysis and industry analysis, comparing a firm's stock to the aggregate market and to other firms in its industry.

Relative valuation should therefore not be used instead of discounted cash flow valuation but alongside it, as together the two types of valuation cover in depth all three aspects of the three step valuation process required to best value securities: company analysis, industry analysis, and economy analysis.

While relative valuation can reveal how the market is currently valuing securities, allowing investors to make comparisons between stocks, it doesn't reveal the accuracy of the market's current valuations. As noted earlier in this book a market can both underprice and overprice securities in the short-run, and therefore the relative valuation model can potentially mislead investors on the relative value of a stock. In order for the relative valuation model to be useful two conditions must therefore be met. First, the aggregate market and a stock's industry must not be significantly overvalued or undervalued. Second, an investor must have a large amount of comparable entities, similar in industry, size and ideally risk, so that any individual stocks which are significantly overvalued or undervalued will stand out, and can be easily identified and ignored in the relative valuation process.

In terms of using the relative valuation technique there are two steps. The first step is to compare the chosen relative valuation ratio calculated for a company to the comparable ratio found for the market and overall ecomomy, the company's industry, and for other stocks in the company's industry. This comparison should reveal whether a company's stock relative valuation ratio is broadly similar to other stocks, or if it is consistently (over several years) above or below these other stocks.

The second step of relative valuation is to explain the relationship between a stock's relative valuation ratio and those of other stocks. For example, if a chosen relative valuation ratio for a stock was found to be consistently above the same relative valuation ratio for other stocks in their industry over a period of many years, then the fundamental factors driving the relative valuation ratio, such as the firm's growth rate, would then be analysed. If the chosen stock's fundamentals were sufficiently above those of other stocks then that could justify the higher relative valuation, and an investor may have identified a superior stock worthy of investment. On the other hand if the chosen stock's fundamentals were not sufficiently higher than those of other stocks to justify a higher relative valuation, then the stock may be overpriced according to the fundamentals, and the investor may have found that the stock is overpriced by the market, and should be avoided.

The next four sections explain different types of relative valuation ratios, and how to calculate them.

6.2 Price-to-Earnings (P/E) Ratio

The price-to-earnings (P/E) relative valuation ratio, also known as the earnings multiplier model, was first introduced earlier in the dividend discount model section, and this section will explain how it is calculated. The P/E ratio is the most popular relative valuation ratio, because it is based around earnings which is what investors care about the most.

An earnings multiplier for a stock can be found by comparing the current market value per share (market share price) for the stock with the last 12 month's earnings per share, with the multiple required to make earnings match price being the earnings multiplier and P/E ratio. For example, if the last year's earnings per share was £2, and the current market price was £20, the P/E ratio = 10. A P/E ratio for the future, known as a forward P/E ratio, can also be found. This is calculated by multiplying the current market price by expected earnings. Whether a current P/E ratio or a forward P/E ratio, the formula is:

P/E ratio
= Current market price / 12 month earnings per share

In order to determine the fundamentals driving the P/E ratio, to assess if an asset is accurately priced or mispriced by the market and make an informed investment decision, the infinite period dividend discount model can be used. The formula for this constant growth DDM was:

$$\text{Value of stock} = D_1 / (k - g)$$

If an efficient market is assumed, where the price (P) of a stock represents its value then this becomes:

$$P = D_1 / (k - g)$$

The forward price-to-earnings ratio (P/E) divides the current market price (P, or P_0) by the next year's earnings per share (E_1), and therefore the above formula can be turned into a formula for the price-to-earnings ratio by dividing both sides of the equation by next year's earnings per share, E_1:

$$P/E_1 = (D_1/E_1) / (k - g)$$
$$\text{Price-to-earnings ratio} = (D_1/E_1) / (k - g)$$

This reveals that the three fundamental factors driving the P/E ratio are 1) D_1/E_1, the expected dividend payout ratio for the next year, 2) k, the estimated required rate of return, and 3) g, the expected growth rate of dividends.

6.3 Price-to-Cash Flow (P/CF) Ratio

As there is a tendency for some firms to manipulate their earnings per share values, some investors may be wary of the price-to-earnings relative valuation ratio, and prefer the price-to-cash flow (P/CF) ratio. A relative valuation ratio focused on cash flow makes intuitive sense when investors are assessing the present values of a stock's cash flows. And a cash flow measure will also be useful for credit analysis when a firm's liquidity and ability to meet its short-term financial obligations is under investigation.

The price-to-cash flow (P/CF) ratio is simply calculated as follows, where P is the market price of a firm's stock, and CF is the cash flow per share:

P/CF ratio = Market price / Cash flow per share

As with the P/E price-to-earnings ratio, this can be a price-to-cash flow value for the present if current cash flows are used, or a P/CF ratio for the future if estimated future cash flow values are used. The specific type of cash flow measure used (e.g. operating, cash flow to equity etc.) depends on what best represents the nature of the company and industry being assessed.

The P/CF ratio fundamentals are the expected growth rate of cash flow, and the uncertainty of the cash flows.

6.4 Price-to-Book (P/B) Ratio

A price-to-book ratio (P/B) is a popular measure to value banks, as most banks assets have a value which equals their book value. Another factor driving interest in the P/B ratio is its potential use in determining more profitable stocks, following a 1992 study by Fama and French which revealed a relationship between a low price-to-book value and an excess rate of return across a cross section of stocks.

The price-to-book value (P/B) ratio is calculated as:

P/B ratio = Market price / Book value per share

Fundamentals for the P/B measure are the factors driving a firm's value, which are the return on equity (ROE) and the cost of equity. As noted earlier the ROE is determined by a firm's net profit margin, total asset turnover, and financial leverage. And the cost of equity is linked to the amount of risk associated with a firm and its stock. The more the ROE exceeds the cost of equity the higher the price will be as the firm is a growth company, and investors will be willing to pay a premium over the book value for the stock. But a lower ROE relative to the cost of equity means the firm's price will be less for investors and is a value stock.

6.5 Price-to-Sales (P/S) Ratio

There are two reasons to consider the price-to-sales (P/S) ratio as a relative valuation measure. First, sales are the ultimate factor driving growth in a stock. Second, sales are more difficult for a firm to manipulate and lie about than other measures such as earnings, cash flow, and book value, and are therefore arguably a more reliable measure.

The price-to-sales (P/S) ratio is calculated by dividing the market price of a stock by the sales revenue per share:

P/S ratio = Market price / Sales revenue per share

The price-to-sales ratio is likely to vary significantly by industry, with retail companies likely to have a far larger sales per share than other industries, and therefore a relative valuation must be between companies in similar or ideally the same industry. And with industry factors being a major determining factor in the price-to-sales ratio, it can be considered a fundamental factor worth investigation in the explanatory second stage of a relative valuation.

www.ingramcontent.com/pod-product-compliance
Lightning Source LLC
Chambersburg PA
CBHW070101210526
45170CB00012B/669